Closing Your Sales

Your Ultimate Guide to Using NLP to Close Sales

Table of Contents

Table of Contents i
Book Description iv
What Made Me Write This Book? vi
Introduction 1
    Neuro 2
    Linguistics 4
    Programming 5
Chapter 1 Fundamental Principles of NLP 7
    Principle 1 Achieving Outcomes 8
    Principle 2 Sensory Awareness 12
    Principles 3 Behavioral Change 12
    Principle 4 Act 13
Chapter 2 The Five-Step NLP Sales Process 14
    Step 1 Establish Rapport 14
        Elements of rapport 15
    Step 2 Ask questions 17
        Interested vs. Interesting 17
        The 80% Rule Applied to clients 18
        The outcome of being interested 19
    Step 3 Establish Value 20
        The outcome of establishing the value 22
    Step 4 Close – Ask for the Sale 22
        The blank order close 22
        The alternate choice 23
        Ben Franklin Balance sheet close 24
        I want to think about it 25
        If you are asked a question 26
        Shut up 27
    Step 5 Handling the Objection 28
        The job of the salesman – Moving the buyer from the point of resistance to objection! 29
        How to handle objections 34
Chapter 3 It's a process – Successful selling 38
    What is the evolving role of technology in selling? 39
    Business-to-Consumer (B2C) sales 39
    Business-to-Business (B2B) Sales 40

Step 1 Prospect and qualify 42
Step 2 Pre-approach 43
Step 3 Approach 43
Step 4 Presentation 44
Step 5 Overcome temptation 44
Step 6 Close the sale 45
Step 7 Follow-up 45

Chapter 4 How NLP Amplifies the Sales Process 47

Develop and refine your client proposition 48
Attitude 48
Sales strategy and process 49
Sales skills 49
Your activity 49
The customer buying cycle 49

Chapter 5 Hypnotic Selling Techniques 52

Technique 1 Mater self-hypnosis 53
Technique 2 Sell them on their dreams 53
Technique 3 Try to paint detailed word pictures 54
Technique 4 Learn instant replay method 55
Technique 5 Make use of hypnotic affirmations 55
Technique 6 Use the power of repetition 56
Technique 7 Narrate hypnotic stories 57
Technique 8 Make use of hypnotic sales scripts 58
Technique 9 Establish trust 59
Technique Use of intraverbal suggestions 59

Chapter 6 The Human mind – NLP information and image processing 61

Secret 1 The mind is primitive 62
Secret 2 The brain loves images 62
Secret 3 The brain loves images of faces 63
Secret 4 Colors inspire specific feelings 63
Secret 5 Names alter behavior 64
Secret 6 Human minds crave a sense of belonging 64

Chapter 7 Useful NLP Tips and Tricks that will help your sales soar in 2020 66

Tip 1 Start before you start & Finish before you finish 66
- Starting before starting 66
- End before you end 67

Tip 2 Go there first 68

Tip 3 Just start talking 70

Tip 4 Use your peripheral vision 71
- Training killer whales 72
- Conscious focus 72

Tip 5 Using the Meta-Model 74

Tip 6 Use the Milton model. 75

Tip 7 Eliminate hesitation 77

One last word 78
Acknowledgments ....
.... 80

Book Description

Are you a salesperson? Are you looking to close sales like a pro?

Well, you have come to the right place.

If you asked any salesperson, they would tell you that there are hundreds of ways to close sales. Most of them still believe in the old school crowd preaching, as well as Colombo closes.

But how many sales can you close this way? How much effort will you have to put in to be spot-on with your target customers?

Not easy, right?

That is why you have to ditch the old school method and start using the NLP technique for sales. One thing that is important to understand is that successful selling revolves around communication, getting what your customers want, and building a rapport with them. Precisely, this is what a savvy salesperson knows that you need to learn. Neuro-linguistic programming offers you invaluable insight into how customers think so that you can tailor your sales to meet their needs and demands. Trust me, with NLP, you can start seeing your sales soar, and your relationships with friends improve a great deal.

Here, we will learn;

- What NLP is all about
- Two fundamental principles of NLP-selling
- How NLP amplifies the sales process
- What the customers' buying circle is like
- Steps to advancing sales using NLP

- NLP approaches that make a difference

So, what are you still waiting for? Come with me, and let's get started to trigger your prospective clients' positive and pre-prepared mental signals so that they are more inclined to buy.

It's time to close sales!

What Made Me Write This Book?

"If I could teach my children only one thing, it would be the skill of selling. Because with that skill, they could be successful at anything they chose for the rest of their lives."

— Howard Ruff, Billionaire, Prominent Author, and Financial Advisor.

My most significant learning in life is that if you don't like to sell or you criticize selling, you are going to struggle all your life trying to sell. That's precisely what happened to me. My first job as a salesperson for a washing soap at 19 years old, I experienced my very first fail! At the time, I earned only Rs 300 (4 Dollars a month).

"If you sell 2000 kg in the first three months, we will allow you to attend the training and make you a permanent employee." My boss told me. I didn't understand the logic. I thought to myself that the only way I was going to sell 2000 kg or more was if I got the training first. Unfortunately, this was their policy. They did not want to waste their time and money training people who are not cut-out for selling in the first place.

I went from one retail shop to another - both big and small - but nobody bought anything from me. I never tried hard. All I did was show them the samples and ask the retail shop owners to make orders. To my shock, they all gave me a big fat 'No.'

The truth is, I did not try hard enough. I did not go the extra mile to ask the retailers questions and pursue their interests. All I did was blame the company that its products have no acceptability in the market - when other sales reps sold tons of soaps every month and earned hefty commissions.

I could never figure out how they do it.

I believed that I could never be an excellent salesman, and I am more suitable for managerial positions.

After about 21 days, my boss called me to his office. I thought to myself that they must have realized that I am more suited for managerial positions. "For the last 21 days, you haven't sold anything, and we are not going to waste three months with you. You are fired!" He said.

I moved on and worked for a garment exporter for two years in production, and I did very well there. This job made me firmly believe that I could never be an excellent salesperson but a good manager.

After about two years, I started my own business, and within seven years, we were very successful and became one of the largest apparel exporters from India. Because this was a sunrise industry, there was no much pressure selling. We attracted so many buyers from overseas who wanted good manufacturers. We would go for fairs and shows, and buyers would come to our booth - if they liked our products and prices, they would place orders. There were no selling skills required.

By 1995, our company came up with one of the most successful IPO, which was oversubscribed 300 times. In the same year, we were awarded a certificate of merit by the President of India. At the age of 60, I decided to sell the company and moved on to be a coach and trainer. We conducted our first training in 2018. In the training industry, you sell your one-day training through Facebook advertisements at a small cost. It's not challenging to fill the room for such a low price at a five-star hotel. That is how we have managed to offer people ten times value for their money and establish credibility and trust in just a day.

Unfortunately, each time I offered advanced courses, I failed because I did not have the guts to look at the audience. I lost most of my clients to our competitors- who had 25% to 40% conversions - and people would run to buy their advance program.

I realized that I needed to do something about it. I went on to take on NLP courses, which helped me understand the advantages of using NLP in sales. Coupled with other trainers' programs, I started realizing massive conversions in my coaching and training - with one of the coaching sessions hitting 95% conversions and 25% in my training programs.

Are you struggling with your sales today? Do you feel like you are not cut-out for sales?

Well, you can change that!

Here, I will share with you my experiences, knowledge, and success using NLP for sales. I am sure this book is going to help you and lots of other people who are looking to boost their productivity. Through proper sales strategies, you can walk away with lots of money in your pocket. You must learn about selling - we all do!

Enjoy reading this book, and I will greatly appreciate it if you can post your review about this book on amazon.

Happy Selling!

Suresh Mansharamani

Introduction

If you have been looking for ways to close sales, then look no further because we have got you covered!

One thing that is important to note is that successful selling revolves around effective communication, understanding customers, and building rapport. While some salespersons may have an instinct for such things, there are so many out there who are wondering how they can do it better. Well, the secret is to learn how to use Neuro-linguistic programming (NLP).

The thing with using NLP is that you stand to watch your sales soar, and your customer relationship improves a great deal.

You may be thinking, "what does NLP mean?" Well, NLP is a technique that was developed as a system of modeling behavioral patterns of specific geniuses in their respective fields of expertise. This technique combines a powerful tool of communication. It offers insight into how people can organize their language, feelings, and thoughts to produce outcomes and actions that often happen unconsciously in various aspects of life.

What is important to note is that buying is a decision, an action, a state, and a behavior. When you couple your skills with NLP, you will be able to communicate in such a way that you engage the thinking of your prospective customers to stimulate their actions, decisions, and behaviors. You aim to influence the state of your clients so that they are converted, and once they make a purchase, they feel good about the choices they have made.

What you need to note about NLP is that it is a broad discipline with an exact methodology, which is correlated with neuroscience, psychology, and linguistics.

"Neuro" represents the nervous system and how humans experience the world using their senses.

"Linguistics" represents how you can determine the particular meaning and the code of language that you experience through your senses.

"Programming" represents the outcome or the behavior that comes as a result of using both the nervous system and language.

At first, this may sound as though it is something technical. However, as you read on, you will realize that everything is so clear. From this book, you will also gain clarity on the importance of engaging clients' senses fully so that you can get 100% attention, and the message is delivered fully.

Now, let us try and delve deeper into the components of NLP and how you can utilize NLP tools so that you are the next superstar salesperson. And if you are already a superstar, you still have room for improvement to steer you towards being a megastar.

Neuro

Did you know that the only way your prospective clients can experience your presentation is through their sense?

While this may sound too obvious, the truth is that this statement may get a little complicated than that when you consider the fact that scientists argue humans are absorbing at least 11 Million bits of data per second using their senses. In other words, most of the information that we consume is usually a result of conscious awareness.

According to research, it is evident that conscious awareness can only process 5-9 chunks of information. This means that as a salesperson or marketing influencer, the best way to tune your clients' conscious attention to your presentation is also to influence their non-conscious attention – something that has a significant impact on their decision-making.

What we mean by unconscious attention is that it carries lots of weight and often includes factors that serve as deep motivators for buyers. They are the key factors they experience from time to time, yet are not aware that they are experiencing these critical pieces of information.

Think about it for a moment, when you are doing face to face sales, your clients can see you – your visual aid and your immediate surrounding. They are also able to hear your voice and that of other people present in the meeting.

Now, if your product is something physical, then it means that your clients can also touch it – whether the actual product, brochures, or other sales materials. Your target client will also have a tactile experience of where they are positioned – whether sitting or standing – their discomfort or comfort. All these things are processed as part of the sensory information.

As you present the visual and auditory content to your clients, they will be able to get the immediate sensations of displeasure, pleasure, and ambivalence – which forms part of their immediate state and subjective experience. You could also add in the sense of taste and smell that may at first seem less obvious but are still present.

All these senses go a long way in forming part of the massive amount of neurological information, one experiences at one point in time and contribute to their decision-making. Your role as a salesperson is to guide your client's senses and steer them in the right direction. This is how you can manage to offer support to both your outcome and theirs.

You may be thinking, "but what if the selling process is done over the phone?" Well, when it comes to phone interactions, your voice as a salesperson is key to capturing the attention of your clients. Here, you have less control over the immediate tactile and visual feeds. This is where NLP comes in to help you!

With the NLP techniques, you will be better positioned to influence your client's visual, emotional, and tactile experience – something that is unique only to NLP selling.

Apart from the external sensory data, there are also internal neural factors that play a vital role in helping the client construct images and sounds based on their past purchasing experiences. The clients will also experience certain sensations in their bodies. Interesting enough, these sensations will indicate to the client whether they are in rapport with you or not.

Linguistics

We all speak different languages based on where we were born and bred. However, what is common to all of us is that language defines how we create personal meaning for our experiences. Most of the information we store and retrieve is in the form of images, feelings, smells, tastes, and sounds. In other words, language allows us to form judgments about something and then communicate to other people our experiences and opinions.

I want you to take a minute to think about all your recent encounters. Out of all these encounters, identify the one you felt an instant rapport and another that you did not build a rapport. Notice that rapport is what you generally experience as a feeling – more like an internal expression.

Realize that language is how you have interpreted and judged the interaction based on what you heard, saw and felt during the exchange process. Take an example where you walk into an art gallery exhibiting art you have never seen in your life. The first thing you will do when you look at the technique is to form a judgment based on your natural preferences/taste built over your life's experiences. In other words, your judgment will be your story.

Language is what offers you meaning and a rationale for the things you experience through your senses.

Programming

This is the automatic action and behavioral response you get from sensory absorption. Note that you run unconscious programs through your system - including those that have occurred through the non-conscious when done deliberately.

When you are selling, you are simply seeking to activate your "buyer's programs." Some examples of programs include asking your client questions, rapport, resistance, agreements, signing contracts, and getting convinced, among others. These are the programs your clients have stored in their behavioral bank. It is important to note that each client has a unique way of running these programs and sub-programs linked with buying.

When you use the NLP selling technique, you will not only be able to engage your client's visual and auditory sense but also build a positive internal representation of purchasing the product. Your linguistic judgment at this point will be along the lines of, "I want this, I must get this," and once you do, you feel good about the purchase you made.

As you read on and uncover more about the power of NLP, remember always to use it ethically!

Chapter 1 Fundamental Principles of NLP

As human beings, we never know the reality. What we do know are our perceptions of reality. In other words, humans tend to respond to life experiences to help in shaping their versions of truth in their minds.

One thing that is important to note is that our neuro-linguistic map of reality responsible for determining our behaviors and attaches meaning to these behaviors is what we compare to reality. In other words, the processes that take place in our minds and within our surroundings are rather systematic. Everything starting from our bodies to the entire society, all interact and influence each other mutually.

That is what forms the basis of NLP – a combination of knowing the outcome, sensory acuity, flexible behaviors, and action.

When it comes to NLP selling, what you must bear in mind is that specific outcomes are most important. Several people do not have a conscious outcome and often wander randomly through life, trying to win sales. However, with NLP, a salesperson must live with a conscious purpose.

If you are going to achieve the desired outcomes, you must act and speak in a certain way. You must use a series of linguistic and behavioral patterns that are effective in helping salespeople change the beliefs and behaviors of other people (specifically their target customers).

Even as you use these patterns, NLP emphasizes on the importance of constant calibration of people you interact with to ensure that your sales approach works. If the approach is not working, you must change a few things or try out different approaches. The main idea here is for you to vary the behaviors until you achieve your desired outcome.

That said, realize that the behavioral variation is not something random – rather, it is systematic. You must be willing to act. Until you take the initiative, nothing will ever happen. In other words, understand that NLP is about thinking, observing, and acting to get all that you want.

Principle 1 Achieving Outcomes

We cannot stress enough on the importance of knowing your outcome. In sales, your main target is to convert prospects into customers and closing sales. The mistake that most salespersons make is going out into the field without a conscious outcome. If you ask most of them, they will tell you everything they don't want but don't have any idea of what they want in the first place. For instance, you should go out wanting to succeed instead of saying that you don't want to fail!

For them, sales are about moving away from everything they don't want. However, if you are going to use NLP in closing sales successfully, you must be ready to move towards the things you want. Realize that without outcomes, then the chances are that you will wander about aimlessly. Once you know what it is that you are looking for, you will start focusing your attention on that thing to ensure that you achieve your desired results.

With NLP, you must have well-formed conditions that your desired outcomes must satisfy. The first condition is that the desired outcome has to be stated in positive terms. In other words, it has to be what you want rather than what you don't want. Your outcomes must be things that you can satisfy. Think about it, if you are given a negative outcome, is it even logical or practical to achieve that experience? The truth is that you cannot engage in the process of "undoing." The only thing you can engage in is "doing!"

For instance, I want to lose at least 50 pounds this year. What do you think of this outcome? It has been stated in a negative state. This same outcome can be stated this way "I want to get fit by the end of this year. I see myself being size Y and able to run 10 km in less than an hour."

The trick is to ask yourself, what do I want? What would I rather have?

Realize that your outcome has to be crystal clear. The fact that you have stated that you want to get fit does not mean that you are clear, even though it is a positively stated outcome. It is vague! But saying that you want to see yourself as to size Y by the end of the year is not only positively stated, but also specific.

The second condition is that the outcome must be testable and verifiable in sensory experience. In other words, for you to close sales, you must have an evidence protocol. If you don't, then it means that there is no way for you to measure the progress of achieving that outcome. With an evidence procedure, you will be in a better position to determine whether or not you are progressing towards the outcome or moving away from it.

The feedback will tell you how you will know that you are on track to achieving your set outcome. The evidence of the other hand points at indicators that show you have achieved the outcome. If you are selling, this could take the form of reports showing that there is an increase in sales figures. It could also be soft evidence of what you see, hear, and feel when that outcome has been achieved.

Let us consider an instance where your goal is to deliver your sales feedback presentation in 2 weeks to the Board of Directors at the Head Office. What you can do is give feedback and evidence before the presentation as you prepare it – feeling motivated, enthusiastic, and excited to deliver it. The feedback and evidence can also come during the presentation – people smiling and nodding as they acknowledge what you are saying. Feedback can also come after the presentation – with people telling you that it was a great presentation and that they enjoyed it, asking questions, and seeking to follow up meetings, among others.

The third condition requires that the desired outcome must be sensory specific. Ask yourself how you would look, sound, or feel like once you close the sales – if that is your desired outcome.

Here, you must act as though you have already achieved the outcome so that you can associate into the experience of having that outcome. This goes a long way in offering your brain a great deal of information needed to represent that outcome in the form of processes – what you see, hear, and feel.

For instance, I want to be confident when selling to my clients. This way, I can make eye contact, feel centered, and seek more opportunities to network. I can hear myself speaking to them in a rick, slow-paced voice and paying keen attention to what they have to say.

The fourth condition is that it must be initiated and maintained by the subject. This sets the locus of control and responsibility for achieving the outcome with you and not anyone else. Understand that the only time it is going to be a well-formed outcome is when you have full control and not when someone else changes in along the way. You are the only one that is responsible for the change so that you can influence the change of behavior in your target audience.

For instance, if you are going to sell successfully, you have to take control of things you can change. Realize that you don't have control over other people – what they think, do, or say. You are going to sell to clients who may choose to be rude to you. Saying "I want to be polite to my clients or sales team" is not a well-informed outcome. However, you can choose to frame it this way "I want to behave in such a way that invites a polite response to my sales team or clients" or "I want to stay centered and respond in an assertive way when my sales team or clients are rude or unreceptive."

Increasing your sales may depend on your sales team or clients. The trick is to offer them guidance, motivation, and inspiration. After this, it is up to them to sell or buy. There could be other factors that come in to play – competition, economic factors, and supplier issues, among others.

The fifth condition is that it must explicitly and appropriately be in context. In other words, every outcome you have set must be universal. There is no way you are going to want "all the time" – it must be under specific circumstances. The good thing with NLP is that there are so many choices created. The aim is not to lower the number of possible choices. The choices must be available and in the right circumstances.

For instance, when you are enjoying delivering a presentation to the Board of Directors and afterward being termed as an excellent presenter, it has the possibility of being aligned with your target and the kind of identity you want to create in the company. It could be that your goal is to be promoted – working long hours, traveling a lot, and widening your customer base. What you need to ask yourself here is, how does this fit with your identity?

The sixth condition is that the desired outcome has to preserve the positive product of the current state. If this does not happen, the chances are that the symptoms substation will likely happen.

Finally, the outcome has to be ecologically sound. Ask yourself what the consequences are for yourself and others. If the outcome is harmful to one or both parties, then stop pursuing it.

For instance, will it negatively impact other people? Will it negatively impact the surrounding? Is it possible that it will impact you negatively? How much time and effort will this have in addition to all other commitments you have, and will that sacrifice affect others as well?

The last thing you want is to achieve your goal and, in the process, open the door to negative consequences for others. This is why the ecology check is the most important and final test to ensure that your outcomes are well-informed.

Principle 2 Sensory Awareness

At this point, you already know your desired outcome. Once you do, the next thing is for you to have adequate sensory acuity. This will help you assess whether or not you are making progress. One thing with NLP is that it teaches salespersons the ability to calibrate or read people.

In other words, once you master the art of using NLP in sales, you will accurately interpret changes in muscle tone, lower lip size, location, skin color and shin, and breathing rate of your target audience. You can use these indications to tell the kind of effect you have on people. It is this information that will help you know whether the feedback you see says that you have a good impact on people or not. Are you able to get people in the desired state?

Unfortunately, what most salespersons overlook yet very important is to know when to stop once you get your target in the desired state.

Principles 3 Behavioral Change

When you are trying to get your prospective clients to buy your product, you must watch your behavior. The secret is to keep changing your behavior until you get the response you are looking for.

If what you are doing is not creating the effect that you are looking for, then you must be willing to change to something different. The trick is to know how to use sensory acuity to determine whether or not your approach is leading you in the right direction or not. If you feel that what you are doing is headed in the right direction, then, by all means, continue down that road.

However, if it is not working, stop and try something else.

Principle 4 Act

Finally, once you know you are headed in the right direction and you have hit the nail on the head, this is your cue to act! Here, there is no space for such phrases as "I don't care" or complacency. What you must understand is that NLP is about acting. You must change your behavior for you and others – now as well as in the future. So, know when to stop and when to act.

Chapter 2 The Five-Step NLP Sales Process

Step 1 Establish Rapport

When it comes to selling anything, the very first thing you must do is establish a rapport with your prospects. Well, the truth is that building a rapport goes beyond what you might be thinking. To master the skill of rapport, you must learn the ability to gain an instant rapport with anyone.

Think about it for a second, you walk into a room, and you don't know where you are supposed to sit, how will you go about it?

It all boils down to establishing a rapport with them.

The same thing applies to sell. You are not going to be selling only to the people you already know. You need to break the horizons and reach a more extensive customer base – composed of different people with different personalities. How are you going to break through to even taking your conversation past greetings?

Rapport, rapport, rapport!

What you need to understand is that most communication will be outside your conscious awareness. According to statistics, it is evident that at least 38% of all communication is a tonal voice, and 55% is physiology. What is interesting is that only 7% of communication is composed of the words we use.

What does this even mean? Well, the truth is that we have a tremendous opportunity that lies outside normal channels – that is what rapport is all about!

The truth, as far as rapport goes, is that the people who are like each other will most likely like each other. On the other hand, when you are bot like each other, the chances are that you will not like each other. This is because, when you like someone from the time you first saw them, you will be willing to assist them in whatever way possible.

Elements of rapport

Speed of processing

This is the very first element of creating a rapport. If you observe keenly, what you will notice is that people often tend to adopt a certain speed of movement. This reflects how fast they process information – whether visually, kinesthetically, or auditorily.

For instance, if you are meeting with someone that is highly visual and you are not there yet, the best thing is for you to sit upright, take a deep breath, and be excited. At least try as much as you can to act in a way that matches with whatever they are doing.

What if the person you are meeting is more auditory? In this case, you will want to slow down a little bit, modulate your voice, and then pay attention keenly. If the person is more kinesthetic, then you have to slow doooooown... and try to talk to them in a way that they can feel it. You can change your tonal voice to match theirs.

Speed matters! Use it wisely!

Mirroring

This implies how you physically mirror another's physiology. In other words, copying their facial expressions, posture, movements, hand gestures, eye movements. This is something that is undeniable to the nervous system and will likely give them the sense that you are more like them.

Voice

The other important element of building a rapport is matching your voice with that of the person you are talking to – tempo, tone, volume, and timbre, among others. It is also essential that you try to match their keywords. For instance, if they like using the term "actually," you can also use it several times in a sentence when talking to them.

Breathing

It is also essential that you try to match your breath with that of your target audience. Match them in and out the same number of times as they do. This triggers them to have the feeling that they can connect with you at a deeper level.

Chunk size

This refers to the size of the pieces of information they use in their speech. Try to match them up as much as you can.

That said, what is important to note is that as you try these elements of establishing a rapport, there is no right or wrong way of doing it. Understand that people vary, and that is just how they operate.

For you to be a master communicator, you must understand that people are communicated with best when you do it in such a way that they can process the information you are giving them. If you notice that someone is quick to understand, try to move fast so that they don't get bored. On the other hand, if you are speaking to someone slow, then chances are that they process information slowly, and you should adopt the same speed – so that they don't miss any critical pieces of information.

Pay attention to the kind of phrases people use. The truth is that these critical phrases reveal what is happening in their minds. As you begin to notice all that, you can now proceed to ask them questions.

Step 2 Ask questions

Note that the first and the second steps in sales go together hand-in-hand. As you establish rapport, you can be asking questions as well. One mistake that most salespersons make is just asking one or two questions for fear that their customers might get tired and move on.

Well, the truth is that you will not understand what your client wants unless you ask questions that go in line with the products you sell. While asking the questions, you must assume that they are going to buy the product. This means that you will be asking questions to find out how they intend to buy it.

This process allows you to ask questions and get one-on-one interaction with your client. That one-on-one comes through rapport and asking enough questions.

Interested vs. Interesting

When asking questions, most salespersons think that they have to keep it interesting for the client. While that might work for you at times, the drill is to be genuinely interested and not interesting.

Think about it; a salesperson of the '50s and 60's; interesting, right? This is the kind of person that would keep the conversation interesting, dress fancy, and would make such a show. However, you would notice that this kind of person is not a friend because he/she is too much – not interested in you!

What is the problem? – they never listen.

If you are going to connect with your client, you must show them that you are interested in them – what they have to say, their interests, and everything that makes them who they are.

The 80% Rule Applied to clients

If you are in sales, what you need to know is that approximately 80% of the people you see have already bought something in their mind's eye. Think about it; someone will not agree to come into your store if they have not yet formed an internal representation of having your product or service. There is a likelihood that they have already imagined having purchased or signed up for what you have to offer.

To succeed in this kind of selling is for you to master rapport and be truly immersed in your clients. For so many years as a salesperson, what I have noticed is that when I talk to my prospects, they will tell me some outrageous things. For instance, I can run into someone at the coffee shop downtown, and when I ask them what their gross sales have been like, their profit margins and how their business is doing, and interesting enough, they will tell me.

Now, the same thing applies to you. You must put together a list of questions. Get all those questions lined up. The way you are going to be interested in your client is when you have the right questions to ask them. Once they tell you what business they are in, the next thing you need to do is ask them questions – how much does your goods cost, what are the profit margins, are you profitable, do you think you are making money, how many hours do you operate every day?

This tells them that you are interested in what they are doing.

If you are selling computers, you might ask them: do you own a computer, what kind do you have? Are you happy with the speed, does it perform unattended processing fast enough for you? Are you part of any user's groups? Do you do any programming? – all those kinds of things!

When you are dealing with a product X, demonstrate that you are genuinely interested in that product. Remember that this is your line of work, and the only way you will show expertise and interest is if you ask the right questions.

The drill is that you stay interested!

The outcome of being interested

One thing you must note is that when you are interested, the chances are that the buyer will forgive anything. You must get the rapport and be involved in earning this. Don't get me wrong, I don't mean that you should do anything, but the truth is that your audience will forgive almost anything.

I have seen salespersons who exert so much pressure on their clients and still go on to use the phrase; "I don't want to put so much pressure on you because you are probably not yet ready to make a purchase, but I believe that this product will offer you the best deal you can get in the market."

After this kind of pressure, the client still goes on and makes a purchase!

Therefore, the very first two steps are; establish rapport and ask questions – but the drill is to be interested – and the buyer will forgive close to anything.

In addition to asking your client's questions, you must find out from them if they have bought anything like the product you are selling before? Did they like it? How do they use it?

It could be that they didn't but precisely what you are selling, but they have something they bought that they were happy about – that is what you need to tap into. This is because it helps them create an internal representation of that item and relate it to what you are selling. This allows you to anchor it.

While doing the anchoring, you must stay as precise as possible. The best trick is to ensure that the questions steer the client towards a greater precision instead of creating ambiguity. The last thing you want is putting your client into a trance.

While there are times when having a client in a trance is useful, keeping them out of trance goes a long way in helping them down the right path. This will help you gain maximum specificity about them and what it is that they want.

Some of the questions you need to ask yourself at this point should be, 'how is it that this client does not have this product?' "is there something that prevents them from having it?"

After which, you can proceed to ask, what is it that they want, what will they see, feel, hear when they have it? How will they know when they have it? What will the outcome allow the to do? Is it only for them? Is there someone else that is involved? Where, how, when, and with whom do they want the product with?

With these kinds of questions, you will be better placed to unravel what your client's meta-programs and values are at that time. Find out from them what their direction, convincers, the frame of reference, and relationships are like. Ask them what their criteria for making a purchase are and what is it that they value around that line of business.

When you know their internal processing strategies at that moment, you are better positioned to break through them later in the selling process.

Step 3 Establish Value

When it comes to establishing value, there three major parts you need to focus on;

- Identifying a need or opportunity
- Establishing the value, the solution holds
- Linking the need or opportunity to the solution

The assumption we are making here is that as you get into communication and get interested, you will easily uncover what it is that the buyer is interested in. Let us consider an instance where someone walks into a health and fitness center. They desire to look better, live longer, and become healthier. In another instance of business consulting, one wants their business to be profitable. When selling computers, you must find out whether your buyer is interested in making their spreadsheets work faster, or do they just want to catch up with the latest technology.

In other words, when you are trying to establish value, it means that you are trying to find a need or an opportunity that your product can meet. Let us assume that you have already identified a need or an opportunity while asking questions – the next step would be to establish the value of the solution you offer to the problem the buyer has.

Finally, it is your job to link the value of the product you offer to the need of your buyer. Note that this is a very important step. Ask your buyer if they see any value in what you have to offer — supposing that your buyer feels that there are not so many people waiting to use computers and that they are always tied up? What you can simply ask them is whether they see value in having their computers work faster.

The way I like to ask it is, "can you see any value to you...?" In this case, the value would be having their computers work faster or having reduced waiting time. It could be that the problem they have is that people often have to wait longer to get on the computer. In this case, you may isolate the problem as the slow printing process. What you can ask them is, "do you see value in having your printing unattended – simply dump the whole system into a buffer?"

The outcome of establishing the value

Now that you have already established what the value is, then the next step is for you to anchor it. In other words, you have to set up an anchor to tie the two together. At this point, the truth is that you have already closed the sale. However, the close here is so inconspicuous that you don't even notice it. You will also need to make use of conditional close and tag questions here, just as we already discussed in the previous step.

Step 4 Close – Ask for the Sale

Now that you have already identified a need or an opportunity established the value of the solution you offer, linked the need or opportunity to the solution, anchored it, the last step is for you to close the sale.

There is a wide range of tried and proven techniques used for a successful closing of sales. Here, we will discuss a couple of procedures that we consider successful and useful when asking your client if the order. Realize that there are just ways you can ask for an order that seems to work magic!

The blank order close

The very first thing you need to do here is to fill out the order form – blank order close. If this is what you are using, it simply means that you have to fill it out while asking questions on the form. Such questions include; what is your mailing address? When should I deliver the product or service? When would you like the installation to be done?

Now, assuming that your client said that they would like to have their computers run faster, then you tell them that their computer or printing system is what makes them wait. If they say it is the printer, then your role is to ask them whether they see any value in having their printers run faster. Then you can ask them when they would like to put in an order for your accelerator boards.

One thing I have learned from some of the most successful salespeople – and the good ones at that – is that they always have the order blank with them during the selling process. This means that once they get the buying signal, they whip it out and start filling it out. For me, the minute I see a buyer get interested, I simply fill out the agreement. Then, once I ask questions that make the difference between buying and selling, I get the agreement form out.

The alternate choice

What you may have noticed above is that the questions we asked did not allow a "No" as a response. This is what is referred to as the alternate choice closing question. With this kind of question, "Yes" is the only possible answer one can give. You can also refer to it as the double bind. When you use this kind of strategy in closing your sale, you must give your buyer an alternate choice to purchase something as you offer them an opportunity to do so.

What this means is that, when the buyer tells you, "The only time I can have it installed is Midmorning hours?" What you can ask them is, "would today midmorning or tomorrow midmorning be better for you?" What you are simply doing as a professional salesperson is offering your buyer an alternate choice.

The good thing about choices is that they are great for when you are making an appointment. You can tell them that you would like to demonstrate the machine to them as you find what time suits them best. You must ensure that you offer your client an alternate choice, in which the answer to either choice is a yes.

Ben Franklin Balance sheet close

This is another specific close that I like. There are instances when selling; the buyer is having a tough time deciding. They are wondering which product or service to get. With the Ben Franklin balance sheet close, you can simply take a piece of paper and write down a "list" of things they stand to gain that ticks all the "yes" boxes.

For instance, in our previous example, we already isolated that the processor runs faster, spreadsheets recalculate faster...You must list at least 8-10 things that they stand to gain from your product or service. This will give them all the reasons why they need to make a purchase today.

Once you have a list, give them the sheet of paper. "Now, I have filled out all the yeses for you, look through, and identify reasons not to make a purchase." What you will notice is that the buyer will be able to come up with no more than three reasons only. How this works is that when one is experiencing difficulty deciding, all the yes reasons that you give them will make them change their minds and make a purchase.

You may be wondering, "Who is Ben Franklin" anyway? Well, Ben was an accountant who used to make out a balance sheet, and on the left side of it, he would put in the word Yes. Under the yes, he listed out all the things he could do and the reasons why he should. On the other side of the balance sheet, he would list out all the reasons why he should not do them. Then check what side outweighs the other.

In the same manner, you should list out all the yeses and then allow your buyer to list out all the nos. You must not help them with the no's because all you are interested in are the yeses. I guess that the no's will be very few, and the yeses will outweigh them a great deal – that will help them know where they need to choose.

I want to think about it

This is another close that I consider very useful and important. When selling to your client, what you may realize is that they are not decided and would like to take time to think about it. Some will tell you, "I want to think about it, or I want to talk to my partner/spouse first." The truth is that this is no objection considering that it is not very specific. What you need to note is that your client is trying to get some time so that they do not have to decide right now.

Think about a Direct mail advertiser; if people don't act on their direct mail within five minutes, this indicates that they have lost you! In selling, if you give your client a long time to think it through, then you are allowing them to get cold feet.

My advice would be once you are in a demonstration and have established value, it is critical that find out from your client whether they are in favor of the product you are offering them. The question is, "are you in favor of it?" The main reason why you are asking them this is because if they are going to talk to someone else who is possibly not in favor of it, how will that help you as a salesperson in the long run?

However, if they are in favor of it first, then they can go ahead and talk to their partners or spouses about it. If they are in favor of it, you can request that all three of you meet together to talk about it. In other words, what you are doing is seeking permission to pitch to their partner as well. Ask your client whether they can arrange a meeting there with you and their partner.

The other thing you possibly can do is that if they have to talk to someone, realize that this may be real or not real. You can ask them to write an agreement with you such that if their spouse or partner does not agree to it, then the agreement is null and void.

If you are asked a question

When you are pitching to a client, it is common to have them asking questions to get clarity on the product. There are instances where the response the question calls for is a yes. In such a case, you don't just say. Yes, and that's all. The trick is for you to respond to that question with another question.

For instance, if your client asks, "Can I have the product in blue?" You can say, "Would you like it in blue?" If your client responds, "Yes," then the truth is that he/she has bought the product already. If their response is "no," then you can follow that with the question "what color would you prefer?"

Request for a proposal

This is also a put-off. Some of the questions that you can ask above and beyond the request for a proposal include;

- Aside from you, are there other people who are involved in this decision-making process?
- If so, when can they get together so that I can give them a presentation of the proposal?
- Would you know what the others want?
- Is it possible for us to talk to them and get their input first before creating the proposal?
- Assuming that everything is okay, when do you think you may want the proposal?
- Is there something in particular that will make them feel good about the proposal during our presentation?

That said, one thing that you need to note is that every proposal often generates lots of questions from the client. The most important thing is for you to ensure that it is tailored to your present client every time.

Shut up

One mistake that most salespeople make is not knowing when to shut up. When you are asking the closing question, one thing that you must understand is the importance of shutting up.

Now, I would like us to go back and define the closing question. What is this? We all have gone through the process of closing, but not once have we defined what it is. Well, a closing question simply refers to any question asked which when you ask, its response is yes and indicates that the client has bought!

When establishing the value, you must pay attention to the closing question, a trial close, and an inconspicuous one at that.

One thing you must bear in mind is that once you have asked the closing question, the next thing is for you to shut up. You should not talk at least until your client has had an opportunity to say something once they hear your closing question. This is a concept that was derived from J. Douglas Edwards – The world's sales trainer up until the 70's when he died.

If you are someone that loves Zen, which I assume that we all are, then you know the power space in between closing question has on the buyer. Most salespeople in their '50s and the '60s are said to be fast-paced in their speech and don't give the listener space. If you are one of this kind, it is important that learn the art of shutting up once you have asked the closing question. If you don't shut up, what you are simply doing is choosing to fail. This kind of silence sucks the buyer into the vacuum of nothingness hence boosting their tendency to purchase.

What you need to note is that the silence that comes after the closing question is what makes the buyer "uncomfortable." This vacuum is what pulls them in so that they can start reasoning as you. If you keep talking, what you are essentially doing is pressuring your client. This is a problem-solving technique – first, you isolate the problem and then uncover that there is value in creating a solution for the problem at hand. Ensure that you demonstrate to your client that you can offer a solution to their problem. For instance, in insurance, the salesperson understands that there is a need to isolate the problem (i.e., retirement) and then offering a solution (i.e., insurance) – this explains why most of them have eventually become financial planners.

Therefore, when closing, there are two major things you can get;

1. You get a "yes" where you finally sign up your client
2. You get an objection

Step 5 Handling the Objection

Now, what happens if when closing the sale, the response you get is a "no?" Well, here are two major ways that you can handle objections. First, you can choose to ignore the objection, something I do the first time, or you can choose to respond to the objection.

Whatever you choose to do, you must establish value in either case. In other words, if you ignore the objection, you must go back to re-establish the value. On the other hand, if you choose to respond to the objection, you must also go back to re-establishing the value.

Here is how this works;

If, after pitching to your client, they tell you, "I can see some value," simply respond to them this way; "Great, let us try and install an accelerator board in your computer." They might respond, "Oh no, I cannot afford that at this time" or whatever else they might say. At this point, you can choose to ignore or respond to that objection. One way you can ignore it is maybe if they say, "Well, I don't have the time..." Or you could respond by reminding them that a while ago they told you that they saw some value in your product. In so doing, you can either get a sale or another objection.

That is your job as a salesperson!

The job of the salesman – Moving the buyer from the point of resistance to objection!

After several years of experience, what I have learned is that the first objection you get from your client is usually not the real objection. That is why you should learn to ignore it.

Now, let us take a minute to think about the latest resistance you have got while trying to close sales. How do you get your client ready to buy something you are selling in the first place? How do you get them to want to buy something that is there and buying something that is here?

You must realize that a lot of resistance usually accompanies the process of selling. One thing you must bear in mind is that if you try to be interesting, then the truth is that you may not be interested enough. This is mainly because you will lack the drive to create a good rapport that will get your clients to get past their resistance. It is that lack of rapport that might get in the way of your client verbalizing their resistance. You must be interested enough to be able to break through that resistance.

What you need to understand is that the first objection is usually not the real reason why your client is not buying. Try as much as you can to talk to them in a way that they get comfortable with you – enough to verbalize their resistance. The trick is always to ignore the first objection.

If at all you choose to answer the objection, respond to it in a way that does not put off your client. Some of the objections you should always look out for include;

- I do not have enough time for this
- I don't have enough money now
- This will not work for me
- I just don't believe you

Responding to time

So, how do you respond to time?

If your client tells you that they don't think what you are offering them is going to save them time or that they don't have enough time to do it, the best response to this is "Well, that is quite surprising Ms. XXXXX because what I am trying to do here saves you time. That is what this is all about. The installation is only going to take 10 minutes of your time. I am willing to come at any time of your convenience. When do you think you will be available? Night or day? Which days?"

Your job as a salesperson is to get your client to visualize, having at least 80% of the product. If you do this, then it means that at least 80% of the time, you have the sale. No matter what happens, if you already have an appointment, consider that you already have 80% of the sale each time. The main reason for this is that your client already has an internal image in their mind. The reason why they are making an appointment is that they already have a mental picture of how that is going to play out.

Take yourself, for instance, when you go out to buy something, it is because you already have visualized yourself selling it. You have already imagined how you are going to make use of that product. This means that if you already have that visual image of the product, then 80% of the time means that you will get an appointment.

Responding to money

So often, we hear clients saying that they don't have money or cannot afford the product you are selling to them. This is another form of objection. The truth is that at this point, you have already established value. Therefore, the most important question you need to ask is why you are getting that objection in the first place when you have already established need.

Well, the answer to this is that you may not have already established enough linkage to value.

Now, you can relate money to time. The trick is to try and ask your client how much money they think it will cost them actually to wait. Try to relate money and time by simply helping them see how much they stand to lose by not solving the problem now.

Another trick is for you always to anticipate the objection that relates to money by setting up a clear contrast between what the imagined and real cost of the product is. For instance, in a health club, once you have established value, the next thing you need to ask is how much it will cost for your clients to have what they want. In other words, what you are asking them is how much perfect health would cost. "It will be worth millions of dollars in reduced medical charges, right?" As you do this, try to set up a contrast. For instance, "Am not going to ask millions of dollars, not even thousands or hundred, because our monthly charges are just ..."

In other words, you are trying to establish the value of the product you have to offer in contrast to what is mainstream. For instance, you are establishing the benefit of being healthy and whole to hospital care costs. Including the number of days, money, and clients you lose at work. The trick is for you to establish value, then re-establish that value in terms of money, the objection, and then re-establishing it in their terms.

If you want your client to be hooked, you must ensure that you demonstrate to them ways in which the decision they make today of buying will pay for itself in the long run. If you are selling business consulting, try to show your prospects how your company will not cost them a dime because they will end up producing more results than the fee you are asking for.

Responding to It won't work, and I don't believe you

Often, we hear clients say that the product will not work for them in as much as it will work for everyone else in the world. What they are simply telling you is that they don't believe you. These two objections are quite similar to each other. What they are saying is that they don't need it. It means that they see the value in it, but for whatever reason they might have, they feel that it will not work for them.

Let us consider a radio advertising niche as an example. You can simply tell your client that the person who owns a well-renowned radio or TV thought the same thing at first but then finally bought your radio advertising. "Look at their brand new; they are soaring over the roof! Don't you want the same thing?"

In other words, if you are going to convince your client to make a purchase, you have to show them specific people who have used your product and services and are have been successful. Show them how happy those clients are. You can even go down to a list of names. Tell them that those people thought the same thing, but when they decided to do the installation or get the product, their problems were solved and are now very happy. "Why don't you call Marvin? Would you like me to give you his number?"

When you do this, you are handing them hard evidence that is hard to walk away from. What is important to note is that if you offer your client hard evidence, then it will be very difficult to get an objection at this point. If you cannot establish the value of the product or service you are selling, then realize that you are gone!

Don't get me wrong – I am not talking about selling your clients what they don't need or want in the first place. The truth is that when you treat selling as a way of serving others, then you won't have to push buttons that are not supposed to be pushed in the first place. You have to ensure that whoever you are selling to is someone that has a need. This means that once you establish the value of having your product, then you have a license to do all it takes to sell them the product.

Without the value, then you are nothing but a hard-sell salesperson. Establishing that they need your product and the value it has to offer means that you are breathing close to closing the sale. Without value established, then all you get are legitimate objections. If you already established value, then the objections you get are not legitimate. Realize that objections are simply buyer's resistances. Your job is to nib them at the bud!

Every objection can be tackled from both the logical and the non-logical side. You can give them both the thinking and the emotional side of things. The emotional side is how you would help them relate to another person that had the same feeling about the product at first until they decided to get it and are now enjoying success in every sense of it.

Notice that, if your client is really into getting more information about the product and the clients who have it already, then it means that they are interested. Now, it is your job to show him the evidence – features. If your client is an emotional type, see through their eyes and get him on the relationship aspect. Once you respond to their objections, again, go back into re-establishing value.

How to handle objections

Earlier, we talked about the four objections that you can get. But the next question you need to ask yourself is how you can handle them. The responses that we have already discussed are quite different from what we are going to discuss here.

We all are emotional, and there are times when we get those clients who are so much annoying and can't seem to understand simple things. Well, as a salesperson, your job is not to tell them how stupid you think they are. "What? Are you stupid? Can't you see that this runs twice as fast as what you have? Do you even know what you are talking about?" Well, this is the wrong way to handle an objection.

I know that YOU would not do that, right? Unfortunately, there are lots of salespeople who do that! They let their emotions get in the way of their job. They try to make the buyer feel like a dummy just so that they look smarter. They think that they know everything, and the buyer knows nothing…

If you are going to handle the objections right, the trick is to follow this process;

Step 1 Listen carefully and fully!

Step 2 Act a little bit surprised

At this point, what you need to bear in mind is that you already have established value. This means that your surprise comes as a result of the objection you get. The trick is for you to repeat that objection so that your client also gets surprised. For instance, if the client tells you, "gee, I don't have the money," you can respond to that as "You don't have the money?"

Just like that, what you have done is feed the objection right back at them. As I have already stated earlier, the worst mistake that salespeople make is that they don't listen – carefully and fully. They don't hear what the client is saying. However, if you take the time to listen carefully and totally, then what you will note is that there are things that the client has not verbalized – but you can see through them.

Paying attention and listening fully to your client's objections will help you see their non-verbalized resistances. This means that when you repeat their resistance back at them, "Is that the only reason you are choosing not to buy?" they will be surprised and feel that there is something more they are losing by not purchasing the product.

Step 3 Smoke out the real objection

When you ask your client whether that is the only reason they are not buying the product, what you are doing is giving them the chance to smoke out the real objection. If it is a fake objection, they will respond, "Yes, that is the only reason I am not making a purchase." At that point, you have him/her. You can then respond, "Oh, so that is the only reason you are not buying."

Step 4 Smoke out a false objection

It is okay to skip this step if you like. However, the most important thing here is for you to try and get your client to agree to you, showing them how to have time. Ask them whether they would buy if you showed them how to have time. This is a very simple process of trying to smoke out false objections so that you can get to the real ones. If they still respond that it is the only reason, it leaves them nowhere else to run off to but to buy!

Step 5 Get right back to establishing the value

It is very important that once you have found out what the real objection is, you try as much as you can to help your client understand the value the product offers. If they say that they do not have enough time, you follow all the above steps we have mentioned and show re-establish the value.

Let us look at this example – highlighting all the above steps;

Objection: I don't have enough time

"You don't have enough time?"

"Yes."

"Oh, is time the only reason why you are not making a purchase?"

"Yes"

"Well, what if I showed you to do the installation, would you be interested? That will not take much of your time."

"Yes, I would be interested."

"Great, I will be happy to do the installation when the computers are not up and running. What time would you be comfortable having me do the installation – night or day?"

When you do this, the client sees all the reasons to buy your product. When you get to this point, ensure that you get right back to re-establishing the value.

Chapter 3 It's a process – Successful selling

"Selling is a skill, and therefore, you can learn how to do it if you want to. The most important part of the sale process is getting your brain set up to attract sales rather than drive sales away."

– Rachel Khor

Did you know that every movie script follows the same basic steps – regardless of genre? Well, it all comes down to the sequence of events. What you will notice is that after a few minutes, the central theme of the movie is re-introduced. After a half-hour of the film, you may see that the main character in the film sets off on a new path, and then shortly after, a symbolic event happens, and so on.

You may be thinking, "Do you mean to say The Game of Thrones, The Fast and Furious and The Notebook all follow the same formula?" The truth is that when you know what it is that you are looking for, you will notice that the whole structure holds up. It is the reason why Hollywood has come to realize that this is the secret ingredient to keeping the attention of the target audience, earning positive reviews and selling, selling, selling!

This is something that applies to any other form of selling, too– irrespective of what product is being sold. In other words, selling follows a logical and straightforward framework that has, for years, been accepted as the model structure. In the same way, salespeople have come up with a set of stepwise processes that they have adopted as the structure of selling – irrespective of cultural and technological evolution. The fact that they have all followed the same fabric for several decades is proof of its effectiveness.

The selling process consists of 7 major processes that you must understand for you to get empowered to satisfy your clients at all times. These processes must be coupled with the NLP sales processes that we have discussed in the previous chapter. One thing that is important to bear in mind at all times is that sales are always a very adaptive process.

While every selling situation is unique, the most important thing is for you to understand what each customer is after and where each one of them falls into the selling process. For you to use adaptive selling, you must thoroughly understand the steps that each selling process follows and how each one of them works so that you can use them effectively.

What is the evolving role of technology in selling?

While the selling process is fundamental and has remained that way for years, the means of communication and how people interact is fast-changing with the use of interactive capabilities over the internet – salespeople and clients alike.

In other words, every step in the selling process requires collaboration between the salespeople and the clients. This is where social networking, among other community-based tools, come in to play. It is through this technology that you can learn more about your target customers every. This means that they will be able to offer the client relevant and robust solutions to their problems during the whole buying and selling process.

Business-to-Consumer (B2C) sales

Let us consider an instance where you are interested in getting a yoga membership. There are good things you have heard from your friends about the new yoga studio in your neighborhood. So, you start wondering in and request to speak to the membership director – who seems to have lots of background knowledge about the Studio and what it is that you are looking for.

You engage in some small talk, and you find out that you both reside in the same apartment complex. The membership director tells you all about the yoga studio amenities, and you are given a tour of the whole facility. You then have a chat over coffee to discuss the pricing options and your preferred payment plan. All the questions that you have are addressed by all the fun alternatives that are available at the Studio.

Once you are satisfied with their response and the offer meets your needs, you decide to sign the contract. Someone from the Studio then follows up with a call to check on whether you are satisfied with the experience at the yoga studio. You fill out a satisfaction survey and get updates on all upcoming events at the Studio.

This is an actual selling situation. You may not have noticed it while reading, but this is precisely what selling is all about. It all follows the seven steps process we will discuss later in this chapter. In the same manner, whether you are buying a yoga studio membership, a house, a car, or a cell phone, the selling process will always follow a similar pattern.

Business-to-Business (B2B) Sales

When it comes to selling, the process of selling is not just applicable to businesses selling to customers, but also businesses to other businesses. It is the same process that IBM, for instance, sells its products and services to corporations, Accenture to consultancy firms or Wineries use to wine shops. As a salesperson, you may call a new restaurant downtown to compliment them for their roasted chicken you had over the weekend. After this, you can ask them whether they are satisfied with their commercial ovens. The chances are that they might be having problems with theirs and your company sells the best ovens in town.

This is how you get the chance to pitch to your prospective clients about your state-of-the-art commercial ovens. This is how you set up an appointment with the restaurant manager, and the truth is that they will be impressed by how much you already know about the business and are also a customer there.

"Does your oven heat up quickly? How is its energy consumption? Does it use energy efficiently?"

When you have gathered this information, it is also essential that you go through their customer reviews, menus, and annual energy costs. After this, pitch to them how your company's ovens are efficient and relate that to an estimate of the yearly savings, they will keep in energy costs if they switched to your product.

But what happens if they are not satisfied with your product? This is where you come in with a no-obligation trial period, show them reviews from similar clients that use your product and reviews on your industry blog, etc. After the agreed duration, you can call them to follow up on the product and what their experience is like. If all good, your client will sign the contract to buy the ovens.

This follows the same selling framework we will discuss in detail. The trick is to ensure that when selling – no matter what it is that you are selling – you do it by establishing value that the client can relate and feel before making the final decision.

The trick is for you to compare the two examples that we have given above – on B2C and B2B, is there any pattern you notice?

The truth is that the products that are being sold may be different from each other, but both situations are adapted and tailored to meet the needs of the customer – following the same steps. There is a chance that you have used these steps before. If not, ensure that you vet your selling processes each time so that you can tailor them to adapt to these seven processes.

Step 1 Prospect and qualify

What do you do as a salesperson before planning a sale? Well, the very first thing is for you to conduct market research to identify the people or companies who might be interested in your product. For instance, you can find the company's information on a local business directory. This is what we refer to as prospecting.

One thing that is important to note is the process of prospecting sets the tone for the rest of the sales process. It is what will give you leads to potential buyers. Prospecting comes from the term "prospect," which means a lead that is qualified, ready, willing, and can buy your product. In an ideal world, prospecting aims at identifying clients who are in the process of or already know what their needs are.

In the example that we discussed above, when you, as a salesperson, calls the target client to discuss the ovens, the most crucial step is to ask questions that will help you qualify your target as a prospect. What you are mostly doing is determining whether or not your target has the desire, the willingness, and the ability to purchase your product or service – an essential component of this step.

You may be thinking, "but what if the target client is not interested in your product?" or "what if they are interested, but their business is facing serious financial constraints and does not have the resources to make such a big purchase?" "What if the person you are talking to is only a manager and not the owner of the business? What if they do not have the authority to make such a decision?"

Well, if that is the case, then they are no longer referred to as prospects. This means that you have to move on to the next lead. The main reason why you are qualifying your prospect first is so that you can ensure that your efforts are focused on people who have a high likelihood of making a purchase. Realize that spending hours of your time discussing the capability of another's company with someone that has no decision-making power or a lead that is about to go out of business is just but a waste of your time. It is fruitful to invest your time on prospects who are qualified and can purchase your product.

Step 2 Pre-approach

This is one of the steps that require you to conduct thorough homework. If you are a good salesperson, then you know that it is essential that you research your prospect so that you can adequately familiarize yourself with their needs. It also goes a long way in helping you learn all the important and relevant background information about them.

For instance, in the B2B example we discussed earlier, the salesperson seems to know relevant information about the restaurant even before they can pitch what they are selling to their prospect. That is how you will approach your prospect prepared and backed up with a tailored presentation.

Step 3 Approach

NLP starts with the first impression that you make. That is what defines how you build trust with your client. Have you ever asked someone on a first date? If you have, then consider that a form of selling situation!

Think about it; how did you get them to go on a date with you? The chances are that you did not just call them up and told them, "Hey, are you up for a date with me on Friday night?" Using such an abrupt method is what turns people off! If you did this, then there is a high likelihood that you did not score the date you were hoping for.

In the same way as a salesperson, it is not right to make the pitch right away. Just as we already mentioned in the previous chapter, the most important thing is for you to establish a good rapport with your prospect first. In other words, take time to introduce yourself to them, make some small talk, ask a few warm questions here and there, and explain who you are and what it is that you represent gently. This is what is called the approach.

Step 4 Presentation

You must take a reasonable amount of time to prepare an exciting presentation before you can even present or pitch it to your client. This is the point where your research will pay off so that your idea for the prospect takes root. By the time you will be presenting your product to your prospect, you must know what their needs are and how your solution comes in to help address their needs.

For instance, if you are a real estate agent selling homes and your prospects are retired older couples, you will not start taking them to see homes with many bedrooms. You will not waste time trying to show them homes with several flights of stairs to climb or a considerable backyard to maintain. You will not even try to show them apartments at a trendy loft in one of the busiest parts of town.

Instead, your presentation should be tailored to the client. Take time to present to them what suits their needs. You can use home tours, videos, product demonstrations, as well as PowerPoint presentations with all the essential amenities that meet their needs. What is important is that you allow your client to look at your product and interact with it. It is this information you share that the client will conduct part of their assessment of whether it is a possible solution.

Step 5 Overcome temptation

Once you make your sales presentation, one thing that you will notice is that certain clients often have hesitations or concerns. These are the objections that we already talked about earlier. This is natural! As a good salesperson, you must view these objections as opportunities to deeply understand your clients and respond to their needs more specifically.

Let us consider an instance where you are trying to convince your friend to go camping with you. Your friend tells you that they would love to come with you, but they have a huge project with a tight deadline. The best way you can still make them come is to say something like, "No problem, my friend, when do you think you can complete your project? I am free next weekend if your project is already out of the way."

In the same way, you don't want to pressure your client. You want your client to know that you understand their current situation and that you are willing to pick up the discussion or the sales once their situation has improved.

Step 6 Close the sale

Finally, once your client is convinced that your product meets their needs, the next thing is for you to close the sale. This is where you give them the sale agreement with the terms of the sale. Then finally complete the transaction process. If it is a yoga membership, they need to sign their membership agreement.

Over the years, my experience has taught me that one has to make several trials closes during the sale process. It maybe you trying to address an objection before your client feels that they are ready to make a purchase. At some point during the sale process, you may notice that the product does not meet your client's needs. This brings you to the most difficult part of the sale process, where you ask your clients whether they are willing to buy. Once the close is a success, this aligns with the purchase step during the buying process.

Step 7 Follow-up

Now that you have already closed the sale, what next? You have sold to your client a car, an oven, or even installed the software that meets their needs. So many salespeople think that their job is done and they are good to move on. One thing that you must understand is that at this point, the client relationship has just started!

This is where follow-ups come in. Follow-ups are an important part of the sales process because it offers assurance for customer satisfaction. You want to retain your customers even once you have sold to them. You also want to attract other new clients. You can do follow-ups by sending a thank-you note, calling your client to ensure that they received the product or even checking in on them to ensure that the product is meeting their expectations and needs.

Today, follow-ups also include logistical details such as signing contracts, setting up installation dates, maintenance dates, as well as drawing timelines. When you do good follow-ups, what you are simply doing is opening yourself up for additional sales, referrals as well as positive reviews. Most Importantly, follow-ups will help open up new opportunities to learn what new customer needs are there so that you can offer them solutions.

Take-home messages

These seven steps are what you need to follow each time you are making a sale so that you have the power to sell successfully.

Prospecting and qualifying require that you search for your potential clients and decide whether or not they have the ability, need, and willingness to buy.

Before making a sale call, you must do your homework by simply researching your client and then planning how you are going to pitch to them.

Your approach is your opportunity to create a lasting impression on your target client by the way you establish rapport with them.

Your research will finally pay off when you make the presentation by proposing your solution to the customer's needs.

View objections as opportunities to deeply understand the needs of your clients.

Once you have overcome the objections, it is high time you close the sale and finalize the business transaction.

Closing the sale is not the end of the sale process. You must follow up with your clients to ensure that their experience with the product meets their needs. This is how you retain them, get a positive review, and land new leads.

Chapter 4 How NLP Amplifies the Sales Process

If you don't yet know, then this is the time to realize that NLP is a great way to amplify sales. It is through NLP sales techniques that you can efficiently boost your revenue and profits.

A friend of mine in UK started her sales career as a retail buyer at B&Q with an estimated budget of $1M. She says that through thousands of sales meetings, training, and calls, she learned so much more about sales based on her buying perspective. These skills saw her grow to become the business development, and strategic management lead of a $billion division at BT – aimed at increasing profit margins and revenue. She currently works with top salespeople to help them not only close their sales using NLP techniques but also increase their revenues.

One thing that is important to note about NLP is that it is great for a wide range of reasons; amplifying sales skills, overcoming blocks, and modeling exemplary performances for knowledge transfer.

So, how can you use NLP to amplify your sales, profits, and revenue flow?

Well, there are five key areas that you need to pay close attention to. These areas include;

Develop and refine your client proposition

This simply means that you need to articulate what it is that you have to offer, your target client, and their characteristics, how they stand to benefit, how you will reach them, their contacts, and how you stand out from the competitive crowd.

Attitude

NLP has so much to offer as far as your state and beliefs throughout the entire selling process. Take a minute to think about the sales beliefs and states that work best for you and then work on them as your starter. Some of the most useful states include; authenticity, curiosity, having courage, determination, open-mindedness, persistence, resourcefulness, as well as being result-oriented.

Start by paying attention to what useful beliefs you have about yourself and your potential client. Believe that you are successful. Take time to rehearse the tough stuff and realize that these are the things that will contribute towards your results. Note that, when you do the right work the right way daily, then you are headed towards getting great results.

The other useful belief you can have about your target clients is the fact that they are going to be successful. Get it within you that they will listen to what you have to say to them and then give them the knowledge you have for them to learn from it and inform their decision-making process.

Sales strategy and process

It is through NLP that you will be in a better position to prospect your clients, qualify their potential, establish value, deal with objections, steer the sales forward for closing and help clients implement and achieve their set goals and meet their needs.

Sales skills

When it comes to selling, the only way you are going to build inner resilience and persistence is when you master the art of NLP. It is; therefore, it is vital that you go through a mental rehearsal, framing, and growing your network so that you are better placed to establish trust, value, and close your sales with success.

Your activity

One thing that is important to note is that sales are like a contact sport. This means that you have to have critical activities planned out for each day. Think of some of the essential habits that you would like to establish and how you plan to review your progress. It is essential that you have plans to improve yourself and what you do.

The customer buying cycle

When it comes to sales, it is so easy to get fixated on the sales process. However, the good thing with NLP is that it will always act to remind you what the purpose of the sales of the process is – helping your clients get through their buying process so that they don't only buy from you but also champion you elsewhere.

The thing with the customer's buying cycle is that it is so simple and obvious. The only issue comes in when you have lots of competition. But what happens when your client is;

- Not sure what their problem is significant enough to address?
- Not sure what the best answer is?
- Has several people who are pertinent in the decision-making process?

Well, if that is the case, the most important thing is for you to do to critically think through what it is that will make the buying process successful in the first place. The truth is that this is very important from the very beginning of the buying process when the client is only identifying what their needs are.

What they are interested in at the initial step is to determine the seriousness of their problem and whether it needs a solution immediately. The truth is that when you jump into a solution too soon, this may stop the sale process. However, when you take the time to identify the implications of possible problems, this will, in turn, encourage the sale process.

The good thing with NLP is that it will help in the first stage of sales, where you have to help the client explore the implications of perceived issues instead of jumping in too quick. Simply look at where your customer is in the buying process and help them complete the stage and move on to the next without placing so much pressure on them.

The five phases of the buying process include;

1. Recognizing what the problem or opportunity is
- *What are the implications of change*
- *What are the benefits of changing*
2. Researching other possible alternatives
- *Identification and assessment of options*
- *Taking time to check recommendations, reviews, and testimonials*
3. Trial

- *Agreement criteria*
- *Assessment*

4. Purchasing the product or the service

- *Hesitation*
- *Commitment*

5. Implementing – by checking both the short- and long-term value

- *Implementation*
- *Checking value*

The other important question you need to ask yourself is who is involved in the buying decision and what their criteria would be. This is something that you need to ask your client. It could be that the budget holder is the one that holds the key to the decision-making process. However, in complex sales processes, it may be the buyer and users that are involved in the implementation process, and that brings you to a final decision-maker being a committee.

In such a case, you should have a champion who will help you drive your solutions internally through various channels and stages of the buying cycle. You must learn how you beat the "blockers" who often align themselves with the status quo or other alternative solutions available.

Chapter 5 Hypnotic Selling Techniques

Did you know that Personal Selling power was the very first business magazine in America? Well, this is something that happened back in 1981 with full-length articles on the science of NLP in the sales and marketing fields. Back then, several people thought NLP was a fad that would come and go just like all the others. However, here we are today, talking and applying NLP in sales because of its enhanced performance.

That said, what many of you may not know is that NLP was derived from indirect or conversational hypnosis. Yes, that is right – hypnosis. You may be thinking, but what does hypnosis have to do with sales? Well, the truth is that this form of hypnosis has nothing to do with tricking people into sleep. Instead, it is a mesmerizing way of talking.

The following features characterize it;

- Grabbing the listener's attention
- Focusing the listener's attention
- Increasing suggestibility

These are the essential skills that you must learn to develop as a salesperson. While NLP uses some of the hypnosis techniques we have mentioned, there is so much more that remains to be discovered. If you are fast enough to master all these, the truth is that you will gain a significant competitive edge in the market.

You may be wondering, "is conversational hypnosis ethical?" Absolutely! This is precisely what salespersons who are termed 'superstars' in the field have been doing. Unfortunately, most of them have not known how they can teach it to others. Here, we have put together some of the most potent hypnotic sales techniques that you can practice to boost your effectiveness and income in sales.

Technique 1 Master self-hypnosis

If you have been in sales, then you know that this is one of the most stressful professions. The truth is that even the most exceptional salespersons get a lot of rejection in their day to day sales activities. Unfortunately, when the times are tough, and there are few sales you are making, it is straightforward to allow pessimism and negative thinking to take over. When negative thoughts play in your head over and over again, you become hypnotized – and that drains your energy.

The good news is that you can learn the art of self-hypnosis by replacing those negative thoughts with positive ones. Instead of thinking, "our prices are too high, we will never make any sale" turn that into "Even though the times are tough, I know that there are clients out there who are ready to buy. I must find them."

I use self-hypnosis, and this has seen me make a dramatic increase in sales and a significant decline in stress levels. You can do it too. Start turning those negative thoughts into positive ones and watch how much deals you close no matter what the economy says!

Technique 2 Sell them on their dreams

The next thing is for you to find out what your prospect's innermost desires, needs, and goals are. Then piggyback those desires, goals, and demands on what you are selling. What you need to note is that when people talk about their dreams and aspirations, they are merely getting into their imaginary world of how their future should look like. In other words, they are abandoning the mundane here-and-now and then traveling into a hypnotic state.

Realize that you don't have to induce hypnosis when people are talking about their dreams in the first place. All you've got to do is make use of the hypnotic state they are already in.

When selling, the trick is to get people to talk about their dreams. Then try to show them that they can achieve their goals and ideal state of living by buying the products you are selling. When you tie their dreams to the product you are selling, what you are merely doing is increasing their likelihood of making a purchase. This technique is commonly used by Charles Givens, Tony Robbins, and all the other superstar salespeople around the world.

Whatever you do, one thing you must not forget is that people cannot resist their dream!

Technique 3 Try to paint detailed word pictures

One thing that you must note is that much of hypnosis is based on mental imagery. This is essentially what I am referring to as detailed word pictures. If you visit a clinical hypnotist, they might have you imagine that you are flying high up on the clouds on a chilly afternoon. This imagery helps you step out of the present moment and concerns and into the power of your imagination. It is this act that activates your creativity, emotions, and mental energy so that the critical part of your prospect is silenced.

According to research, it is evident that most of the superstar salespeople use lots of imagery as compared to average people. When selling, you can do the same – use mental pictures after the other in your presentation. It is not only positively mesmerizing but also offers you a competitive edge in the market.

Use it wisely; you have all the power!

Technique 4 Learn instant replay method

Let us consider an instance where you are selling a car. What is the first thing you need to do when you find a prospect? Well, the trick is to find out how they bought their last car. The same applies to every other product you are selling – whether a home, appliances, or gadgets.

Whatever it is, the first thing you need to do is ask questions and pay attention to what your prospect has to say. This is what will help you learn every mental step they experienced, the order of their spiritual steps, and who they consulted in their decision-making process.

Realize that when people talk about how they have made past purchases, they often get taken by their own stories. Because we all are creatures of habit, there is a high chance that the present purchase we make is made in the same way as the last one – however long that may have been. If you are selling them a house, sell them in the same way they bought the previous one. If it is a suit, do it the same way as the last. When you do this, you are making it hard for them to resist you because, in so doing, they will be resisting themselves.

What is interesting is that people find it very hard to resist their thinking, values, and principles. The truth is that they will not even know why that is happening, but they will find it mesmerizing to buy the product from you. They will find the process to be effortless based on the fact that it perfectly fits with their preferred way of buying.

Technique 5 Make use of hypnotic affirmations

Do you find yourself talking to yourself sometimes? Well, that is not strange because we all do, one way or the other. According to research, it is interesting is that several people talk to themselves at the rate of 500 words/minute! If you are going to be talking to yourself that much, isn't it a great chance to say something positive?

Several of the old-fashioned methods of positive thinking have neglected the role of using positive affirmations in self-programming. Think about it for a second; if you use positive thinking in selling, what would your attitude be like? Each day, you are talking to yourself about what sale means. The trick is to ensure that whatever it is that you are saying about it is positive. If you go about your job thinking about how selling is such a drag and wondering how you got yourself in that field, then the chances are that you will never close any sales.

I have learned to use hypnotic affirmations to get rid of all the negative thoughts. You can start today by repeating the following affirmative statement at least 100 times each day or any chance you get – "I love selling, selling is such an easy task for me. It helps me get to meet new people." "The company I represent is great, and the products I sell are such an incredible line."

When you continuously do this, these positive hypnotic affirmations will get you in a positive mental state, which will impart self-confidence no other competitor can shakedown.

Technique 6 Use the power of repetition

The power of hypnosis comes significantly from repetition. It does not matter whether the repetition is a swing of a shiny gold watch or the use of such words as "I'm great" or "calm down." To be a sales superstar means that you are not afraid to repeat yourself – especially if you are making a critical point or a new one at that.

If you are going to keep what you do as fascinating as you like it, then it means that you have to master the art of repeating it each time. Each time, try to say the same thing with a little twist. Whenever you use repetitive, hypnotic statements, follow it with something else and then go back to it again and then something else. My mentor always told me that part of the reason why they are very successful in sales is the fact that he learned to repeat hypnotic statements each time when setting new sales records.

For instance, "You are going to love this product. Trust me; you will love it. You will love this forever." These are just examples of statements you can use.

In sales advertisements, there is a belief that "nothing sells like repetition!" This is precisely what you should be doing. Think about it – if you are selling sports ads on the radio, you cannot possibly hit your target with just one or two advertisements. Look at all the products that you have, would you have bought them if you just heard about them once on a TV or radio advert? Not!

You may wonder, "why is repetition important in the first place?" The truth is, there are millions of people who are terrible listeners. In other words, 80% of what is said is missed each time, and they pick up only 20% of it. If you don't make use of hypnotic repetition in your selling, then you risk not having your prospects hear the most crucial part of your messages.

Therefore, if you have factual or emotional messages that you would like to share with your prospects during the sale, then start doing that – they are powerful when coupled with hypnotic repetitions.

Technique 7 Narrate hypnotic stories

Stories and metaphors are some of the most powerful hypnotic techniques of all time. What you will notice is that when people listen to a story, they let their guard down and are less critical. In their minds, they are "seeing a movie."

In sales, when you employ the technique of a hypnotic story or metaphor, people tend to think that you are not selling – when you are making the most important sales point of all time. The trick is for you to ensure that before you start selling, you collect some of the most effective sales stories, write them down and practice, practice, practice. By mastering these stories, you stand to increase at least 20% of sales or more.

Technique 8 Make use of hypnotic sales scripts

'What are hypnotic scripts?" you ask. Well, these are simply an organized collection of words that are hard to forget. Some of the hypnotic scripts that we already may be familiar with are "To be or not to be ..." "ask not what I can do for you..."

Unfortunately, most salespeople already know most of these scripts, but they fail to use them in a way that is interesting to the listener. They use them in a dull and banal way. If you are one of them, then the chances are that this is the reason you are not getting even an appointment. It could be the reason why your prospects try as much as they can to avoid you. The most important thing is for you to try and practice using them in ways that are fascinating and mesmerizing to the clients. When you do this, you are making it hard for your clients to ignore you.

As a salesperson that people find exciting and mesmerizing, you will command the attention of millions of potential clients across the world. I know a friend that has done over 50 radio talk shows across the globe. He tells me that he figured out ways he could talk about selling that mesmerizes a big audience. In the same way, you can find powerful combinations of words that positively opens people's minds up to the products you have to offer.

When selling, what you have to understand is that objections are entirely predictable. Therefore, before you set out each day to sell, predict every objection that your prospect might raise when trying to buy your product. Then find solutions and couple them with mesmerizing, mind-blowing, or heart-stopping hypnotic scripts that will take power out of their objections. This way, you will eliminate not only objections, but also close sales successfully.

Technique 9 Establish trust

According to research, it is evident that we can only trust and like the people who like us. One of the fastest ways you can build trust with someone is using the pacing technique – matching or mirroring techniques. In other words, you look at your client and try to be like them, act like them, and talk like them.

When you pace your client, the good news is that you lower and dissolve your differences. You make it difficult for your client not to like you because if they do, they are choosing not to love themselves.

Just as we already discussed in the previous chapters, the essential way of building rapport with your client by aping their speech volume, rate, emotions, beliefs, values, opinions, moods, and body language, among others. The thing with pacing is that it triggers the effect of positive hypnosis. When you do this, you get to the point where you can tell what your client's thoughts are and what they are likely to say next – that is how you earn power and self-confidence in selling!

Technique Use of intraverbal suggestions

The intraverbal suggestions simply come from voice inflections and intonations. For instance, when a hypnotist uses the word "glad," they will just pronounce it with a soft, deep voice saying "gllllaaaad." The term "happy" would come put as "haaaappy"

What you need to realize is that when you use such voice inflections and peculiar intonations, what you are doing is giving the word extra power. As a sales professional, you must leverage the power of tones and inflections. These words will trigger a strong positive emotion in your prospect. Otherwise, if you say the words in the usual way, they will not have much effect. Realize that your distinctive voice inflections and intonations are what make the difference.

Today, start by going over your sales presentation and telemarketing calls to identify some of the keywords you can use intonations and inflections on. Using interverbal suggestions when saying these words is what gives them more power. Try using different combinations of inflections and tones until you get one that works perfectly well and brings out the desired effect in your clients.

That said, you must make use of these ten techniques when closing sales. It is these ten techniques that most of the top seasoned salespeople swear by for making billions of dollars sales. This art of hypnosis is what NLP is all about. NLP is what makes you persuasive and gives you an edge over your competitors – which is why you will close sales with less effort.

Come on, give hypnosis a shot, and you will be amazed at how much sales you close.

Chapter 6 The Human mind – NLP information and image processing

You may be wondering why we are talking about the human mind, and it processes information; and its significance in NLP. Well, the truth is that NLP is all about the human brain. When you know how the human brain operates – processes images and information – then you are better placed to put that knowledge into good use. It is this skill that will help you become an effective marketer and seller.

Today, there is ongoing research that is aimed at figuring out how hard-wired human preference affects their way of making decisions. In other words, NLP has given rise to a field of research termed "Neuromarketing," which refers to the systematic approach of collecting and interpreting neurological and neuro-physiological insights about the buyer using a wide range of protocols. In other words, you try to use nonverbal and unconscious physiological responses to different stimuli for selling or marketing of products.

Take a minute to think about how this area of research influences your brain and behavior to respond to marketing and selling – whether consciously or unconsciously. The truth is that there are cognitive biases that are built into us all. We cannot help it. When you are selling your products to a prospect, your marketing will either align or work against these cognitive biases.

You must learn to understand these predispositions so that you know how the mind processes information and images. Realize that the world of sales is full of competition for attention – a fierce one – and knowing what lights up your client's brains gives you an edge that will help you win.

Here are some of the secrets you can tap into to get a perspective;

Secret 1 The mind is primitive

According to research, the part of the brain responsible for controlling reactions and emotions called the amygdala works faster than the conscious or the rational mind. This is what you get your gut feeling from, something that happens in less than three seconds. Note that your emotions make a lasting imprint as opposed to the rational mind.

Therefore, when you are selling to your prospects, you must aim for that gut feeling. Pay very close attention to how your materials are scanned – fast or deliberate – because no has is inclined to do that anymore. What is it that your client sees first? If you are making your sales online via email, then what your client is likely to mind first is your subject line or header. Does it grab the attention of your prospect? Does it speak to their pain, needs, wants, and emotions?

Set aside as much time as you can to draft a selling headline. Make your presentation welcoming and easily grokked. This leaves an impression on your prospects and determines whether or not they will be interested in your product or not.

Make it worth their time!

Secret 2 The brain loves images

Did you know that the human mind processes image much faster and better as compared to texts? According to research, it is evident that at least 90% of all the data the human brain processes is visual. When you attend a presentation, you will tend to remember pictures with texts much more than texts alone, right?

This is what also works in NLP sales. When you are pitching to your client, learn to use as many images as you can, and make them unique. Lay off those stock shots! For instance, if you check any good Hotel and resort, you will notice that they have integrated candid guest images into their "Travel for Real" campaign.

This is how you can also make your selling process enjoyable to the client – enough to get them to make purchases. People are drawn more to beautiful images or visuals. You can learn to use Over (a mobile app) or Canva to create custom images that specifically and primarily speaks to your prospects.

Secret 3 The brain loves images of faces

From research, it is evident that natural selection favors humans who can identify threats fast and establish relationships. As part of that, the human's mind is wired right from birth to recognize and have a preference for the human face. The role of the brain that is responsible for processing human faces is close to that responsible for processing emotions.

Therefore, when you are selling products and services to clients, you should consider incorporating human faces on your presentation, brochures, and website. This is what is going to drive the desired action among your prospects

According to eye-tracking studies, the human brain, by default, chooses to look at human faces first in what you have to offer. You also will notice that people look where the faces are looking. Therefore, try to entice your clients by adding faces that look at the call-to-action button or the essential part of your sales message.

Secret 4 Colors inspire specific feelings

Did you know that there is more to color than what looks good? The truth is that different colors stir up mixed emotions and signals in the brain. According to research, between 62 and 90% of the senses we have about a particular product is determined by what color they are. When you see yellow, this tends to activate the anxiety centers of the brain. Blue, on the other hand, established warmth and trust. Red creates a matter of urgency, and so on.

You must note that there is a science and art behind the choice of color you go for – especially when it comes to the products you are selling or how you design your call-to-action message or button. You must not choose colors arbitrarily. Take time to study your clients and learn what colors they would prefer, and then offer them the product in that color. The best approach you can give is always to test the different colors and the responses they bring before you can set out to sell.

Secret 5 Names alter behavior

The name you call your products often affects how people react to it. According to a study conducted by David R. Just and Brian Wansink, Cornell University – Food and Brand Laboratory, calling a similar portion of spaghetti "double-size" rather than "regular" goes a long way in causing diners to consume little pieces.

In the same way, when you are selling products and services, be very careful about how you name them and the kind of wordings you use. The names or wordings you choose have a significant influence on how your clients respond. Always go for model descriptions when creating customer-oriented messages.

Secret 6 Human minds crave a sense of belonging

The human brain has an innate desire to conform. According to research, it is clear that where people are free to do what they like, the chances are that they will tend to imitate each other.

When selling, you can get anxiety out of the way, signal belonging, and establish a strong sense of credibility by using social proof and signals – in the form of endorsements. Make use of well-known influencers in the market, customer testimonials as well as social widgets when selling.

It is essential that you also use a specific language on your call-to-action so that you can signal a call to confirm. Instead of telling people "sign-up for newsletters and updates," tell them, "We are the world's leading resource for home appliances." Instead of asking them to subscribe, ask them to join millions or thousands of other contractors and homeowners who seek home upgrades every day.

That makes the whole difference between closing sales and getting an objection.

NLP is everything!

Chapter 7 Useful NLP Tips and Tricks that will help your sales soar in 2020

Tip 1 Start before you start & Finish before you finish

I loved the TV show, 'Inspector Morse.' Every week, our opera-loving hero made use of his reasoning, intuitions, and the power of observing the human condition to solve impossible mysteries and bring all the villains to justice.

Whenever someone told a story, Morse had mastered the art of getting beneath the story to get the real story of an event. The strategy that stood out was that of terminating interviews. He would say, "Well, that covers it all" then he would get up and leave. The person being interviewed would feel much more relaxed, and at the door, Morse would be like "One more thing though..."

Well, don't get me wrong – I am not suggesting that you get on your client's neck. However, you can use this strategy, especially when people's armor is off. This is when their defense is already down. The best ways to accomplish this is by;

Starting before starting

Once you have made your introduction during sales, you can say things like, "Before we can get started with the sales presentation, there are a couple of key things I would like to cover..."

Then you can proceed and start!

This way, you help your prospects to let down their armor ahead of the "formal" beginning. Personally, there are several instances where I have done my pitch at the pre-beginning session and closed sales there.

End before you end

Here, just like Morse, you can finish before actually finishing. In other words, if you are experiencing difficulties getting to the critical point, you could use phrases like "Well, I think that is all for now..." then get up to leave. However, before actually leaving, you can say, "Oh, one more thing, though ..." and then begin again. You will be amazed at how attentive and responsive your prospects get. They may suddenly have questions about the product, the buying process, and so on.

One thing you need to bear in mind is that when you take people literally, you create a mental image of yourself and the product you are offering. Remember that the human brain is always goal-seeking and will always move towards the goal you put it into.

For instance, if you are selling products for weight loss, the last thing you want to do is pitch by saying, "do you want to lose weight?" The truth is that people don't like 'losing' things. When you put something in the negative, the brain has a different way of processing that message. Since childhood, we have all been conditioned not to lose things but instead find them. Start your opening with such phrases as "Do you want to be slim, fit and healthy?" This helps the client to imagine themselves just like that – slim, fit, and healthy, and who wouldn't?

You will realize that your clients' faces begin to brighten, and eyes fixated on you and attentive to all that you have to say. They will start to see themselves just the size and shape they want to be, looking so good and hearing all the appreciative comments that others tell them.

The trick here is to help your client set definite goals and achieve them by purchasing your product. When you take people's literacy, they will give all the essential pieces of information about what is going on within them. This is precisely an example of what Richard Bandler once said, 'people will tell you all you need to know in the first minute.' Of course, you are not going to get this kind of openness when you are uptight with your clients. You have to be open and ask the right questions in the first place.

This is your secret to being good at NLP, use it!

Tip 2 Go there first

One of the best ways you can think about NLP is the process of helping others move from their present circumstances to their desired situations. One way you can achieve this is by offering them access to a set of necessary resources that will help them make that transition.

The essential resource here is the power of the individual state of mind. While the human body and mind are one system, a combination of the two with a person's feelings and thought process is what makes it a state. Think about it for a second; if you are soaking in a hot bath, the chances are that you are in a different state of mind as compared to when you are running, giving a presentation, or kissing your crush for the very first time.

One of the powerful NLP skills is the ability to guide your clients into different states. It is this ability that makes communication and changes possible. If you think of trance, for instance, that is an emotional state, just like gratitude, happiness, and love. The thing with emotional states is that they are very infectious. In other words, if you want your clients to have a specific feeling, then the trick is for you to go there first.

If you want to get a punch on the nose, then you have to start disturbing someone. If you're going to paint a smile on someone's face, it is if you start distributing it to them. Whatever state you want your clients to be in, just go there first yourself.

You may be wondering, 'how do I go there first?' Well, there is a wide range of ways you can achieve that. As you start practicing, you will begin to unravel more approaches that effectively work for you. Here are some;

The fastest and easiest way you can change your mental state is to change your physiology. For instance, if you want to snap out of undesired states, you could start by jumping up and down, beating your chest, or shaking your hands, among others. By this token, you can activate your desired state by adopting a specific posture or stance. Soon, you will start experiencing the sensation of that very state of mind.

Fake it until you make it is another way to get people to feel the way you think. When you are selling and want to trigger a certain feeling or state in your audience, then start by pretending that you already are in that state. Pretense tends to trigger the nervous system to get that idea fast enough, and before you know it, the state will start manifesting. Realize that the more convincing you are, the more you get people there too.

Finally, anchor it. This simply is a representation in the human nervous system that triggers other images. It is much like Pavlovian conditioning. This means that when selling, you can choose to anchor yourself intentionally. For instance, you can pin that state by thinking of an occasion when you had an enjoyable or pleasurable experience. Then see what you saw then, heard and felt. As you begin to have that sensation and let it increase in intensity, squeeze your thumb and fingers of your left hand and release them. Then finally break that state by interrupting it with something else such as what you had for lunch the previous day. Then press your thumb and fingers again for the state to come back.

If you practice this over and over again, you will be able to get the state you desire fast and influence your prospects into that state too. The truth is, when you have established a rapport with people, you can go into a state you want, and they will follow suit.

Tip 3 Just start talking

One of the things that I love most when training students on NLP is to get my students to play with Ericksonian Hypnosis cards as well as Irresistible Influence Cards. This is one of the best ways you can raise people's energy, create a fun learning environment, and rating the skills they develop.

However, there is always a challenge one has to overcome before the skill starts to take off.

The thing is, most people want to know what it is that they are going to say before they can even say it. Just like language generation, grammar, and word selection, the unconscious automatically produces language. Think about the last telephone conversation you had, what is the likelihood that you were consciously thinking of what words you will say next. Did you think of them at all? Did you think of how to structure the sentence? Did you think of where to place the verbs?

There is always a goal in your mind that you have set, whether consciously or not. The unconscious finds the right phrases, words, and sentences to steer you forward to it. The key to being fluent with the language pattern of NLP is practice, practice, practice. This is what will help you integrate everything necessary at the unconscious level, set communication goals that suit your prospects, and then start talking. When you do this, the patterns begin to automatically and spontaneously emerge.

When it comes to learning the hypnotic language, you have to be willing to make mistakes. When you were a child, before you learned how to speak, you did not have the concept of failure. All you did was an experiment, make sounds with your vocal cords and mouth, and then pay attention to the response you got. This is precisely what happens when it comes to hypnotic language – you let yourself make mistakes and learn and grow from them.

First, set communication goals you wish to achieve when interacting with your target audience. This way, you are triggering your unconscious to produce words and phrases that align with your set goals. If you have not set any specific purpose, the chances are that your unconscious will pick whatever has been rattling in your mind.

For instance, when you are listening to issues your client has been experiencing in their business, your mind will stay aware of a new range of possibilities, and that will start generating solutions. That, in turn, gives you a sense of confidence as you repeatedly practice these patterns.

One of the phrases you can capture your client's attention includes "what happens when you..." if you want to find out how your product can work for your client, you can use this phrase. This way, they start to imagine all the benefits they stand to enjoy by using your product or service.

Today, take time to set the goals for your sales communication, read the patterns out aloud even when you are not consciously aware of what you are saying. What you will realize is that the unconscious will start filling them out for you. Don't try too hard to be perfect the first time. Enjoy the process of getting better with practice. The fastest way to learn anything is to do it!

Tip 4 Use your peripheral vision

According to the co-founder of NLP, John Grinder, the three main obstacles to mastery of any given skills include;

- Over-reliance on focal vision
- Hesitation

- Internal dialogue

What you need to understand particularly about NLP is the fact that it relies hugely on your ability to perceive a more comprehensive view of things and then act instinctively on them. When you identify ways to get rid of these obstacles, only then can you start to increase your ability. One of the fastest ways you can close sales and get the results you desired is by paying attention to your peripheral vision.

Training killer whales

A couple of years ago, I met a killer whale trainer that told me about her experience doing what she does. What she told me was that she exercises caution whenever she is working with certain creatures to avoid reinforcing the wrong thing. Most creatures spend most of their day watching and listening. They don't have an internal dialogue, but they take note of everything. They take note of all the patterns that killer whale trainers don't because of more attention. If they notice a trend that the trainer has not reinforced, they leverage it to their advantage.

How do they take note of these things? – using their peripheral vision.

You can do the same as a salesperson. Look around you and learn what other sharks in the industry are not doing and then use that to your advantage.

Conscious focus

What you are presently using to read this book is your focal vision. It is through the small, critical elements of your visual field that helps you see the difference in fine details. Unfortunately, some people over-rely on their focal vision to the extent that one might think it is connected to their conscious mind.

The peripheral vision opens you up to what is both above and below – it is what helps you detect movement in your surroundings, and you can think that it is linked to your unconscious mind.

Let us try this practically;

As you keep reading, try to focus your attention on the beginning of the sentence. As you keep looking at the first word, try as much as you can to relax your gaze so that you are aware of the edges of the page. How much can you perceive on each side?

This is what we call – peripheral vision.

When you make use of your peripheral vision when establishing rapport with your client, the good news is that you will derive more information about the – one you wouldn't have access to in the past – blink rate, breathing rate, and gestures among others.

This goes a long way in helping your unconscious mind to get on the act and stir up intuitions about your client - so that you know what is going on inside them.

Now, try to sit in a relaxed position, paying attention ahead. Try to imagine having an extra set of eyes on your belly button. What sensation do you get on your skin at the belly region? Imagine yourself looking through those belly button eyes. When you do this, you will start to notice your peripheral vision opening up. If not, that is fine. You can try this tip instead;

Simply assume a relaxed sitting position and pay attention ahead of you. Imagine that you are seeing an orange floating a couple of inches above your head. This will start to open your peripheral vision so that you can view the world with a more relaxed gaze. Practice this over and over again until you can get it right.

When you are talking to your client, you can also go into peripheral vision. This will help you become aware of things that you would otherwise not be aware of. As you get more connected to them, you can use that to sell them your product in a way that is more comfortable for both of you. This will help you take note of their signals, expressions, and gestures when they think that you don't see them. These signals will go a long way in helping you know what it is that they are interested in, and you can go right in and give them that – just like you read their minds!

Tip 5 Using the Meta-Model

This was the very first NLP development created by both Richard Bandler and his partner John Grinder, 1975. It is this particular model that formed the basis for other discoveries in this field.

The meta-model works on the principle that people don't experience reality directly. Instead, they experience reality through such things as maps of reality that they create in their minds. When your client tells you that they have a problem – or any other person for that matter – the truth is that they don't have a problem or challenge. It does not exist typically in reality. It is only a map that exists in their minds and perceives it as reality. This means that you can use that trick to enrich their maps so that their perception of the world is richer. When you do this, you are solving their problems or helping them overcome their challenges.

This model has been perceived by so many people to be the most difficult NLP technique. Now, to understand this model better, I want you to imagine that you are selling your product to your target clients – people who have a problem or limitation for which you are offering a solution. First, think about how you manage a problem. That is the question that is going through your client's mind.

The most crucial point to note is that when a person takes responsibility for their circumstances, that is the time when they begin to tap into the power of changing their situation. When you ask such a question, the person will presuppose that they are skilled at addressing the issue. How do you manage to stay in debt? How do you manage to drive a car without a comprehensive insurance cover?

When you ask your client this question, you are getting them to believe that they have a skill, and that makes it possible for them to learn another skill – one with the solution. That is what helps you get your client to have a structure of their subjective experiences. You get to tell your client that what they are experiencing is something that someone else has experienced before.

When selling to them, simply ask them the question and listen. The chances are that they will give you clues on how they have created an internal representation of their problems or challenges. You will see their eyes move, gesture, and body language will tell a lot. The truth is that no one ever thinks of their problem as a skill. When you give them this change of perspective, they get so much power in their situation and will want to hear the solution you've got to offer.

While using this technique, bear in mind that rapport counts a great deal!

Tip 6 Use the Milton model.

Just the other day, I searched for something on Google and got about 7000 references to it. Some of them were images, and others were complete documents. Some of these references were more relevant than others – which got me thinking about how we process language.

When you first hear a word, the unconscious mind will sort through the whole internal reference to find that word and its meaning. This is a rapid process that we don't even notice it taking place in the first instance.

Let us take an example of a sentence like, "The apple fell from the tree." For us to make sense of that sentence, the unconscious mind will try to search its internal reference for the terms; apple fell and the tree. But when you hear this sentence, it immediately makes sense, but you were not even aware that the search took place.

Well, the basis of this internal search is what forms the basis for hypnosis and how it works. The Milton model is all about using language to get the same results as the Erickson's approach, in which he spoke in an artfully vague manner. For instance, if someone says, "Your feet feel relaxed," you may respond by saying, "No, they do not." However, if they say, "This will start to make you feel certain sensations at this part of your body," the chances are that you will start noticing them.

You can use this kind of technique when closing sales to pace your client's experience and lead them in a new direction you want them to go. With this, you can get your clients to covertly do things they usually would resist if you asked them to do them overtly. This is precisely how you get access to the extraordinary power of the unconscious mind.

Think about it this way; you are reading this book for a reason – you want to learn something. This means that you also want to discover how you can put those new things you learn into practice. Now, if you reread this sentence, you will notice that it is vague. Everything I have said about your experience is a guess about your experience, right? In the same way, you can use this trick with your clients. The truth is that people like there to be a reason for everything – to make the world sure. When you do this, you get people to say yes. Using language in this hypnotic manner tends to have a significant influence on people.

That said, some of the business essentials you must demonstrate while closing sales include; integrity, honesty, leadership, diversity, innovation, and creativity. Try telling your prospects that your commitment to change is your source of effectiveness. The truth is that when people hear this, they tend to get spaced out. The key is to use your language skillfully and intentionally

Tip 7 Eliminate hesitation

Richard Bandler said, "whoever hesitates waits...and waits...and waits." Each one of us, at some point in life, has been in a situation where we have wanted to do something but have found ourselves hesitating. This is a significant barrier to learning, and you must overcome it if you're going to win clients and close sales.

Just take a minute to go over your sales experiences; are there times when you have experienced sales reluctance? Realize that you cannot ask your client to do something that you don't want to do in the first place. Today, choose to go for it. Approach that client that you feel unapproachable and pitch to them. In sales, if you are going to make a win, then you have to eliminate hesitation. Decide to set out each day and make an absurd request while keeping that straight face. Look for situations where you have hesitated in the past, and don't hesitate anymore. Start doing them and enjoy every response you get.

You may be thinking, "how does this even work?"

Well, so many of us have been conditioned against making any mistakes. However, if you want to be skilled at NLP and use it to win sales, then you have to eliminate hesitations and unhelpful responses. While there are times when it is helpful to hesitate, know that there are so many other salespersons out there who are chasing the same opportunities and clients like you. If you dilly dally, then chances are that you will never be able to get desired results.

One last word

Indeed, it is evident that NLP reflects the principle that a human being is a connection of the mind and body coupled with consistent and patterned linkages between neurological processes as well as adopted behavioral strategies. One thing that is important to understand is that NLP is all about interest in the manner in which people communicate and create experiences through their behaviors and thought processes.

In sales, NLP goes a long way in helping people create desired and useful experiences in the world. It is through NLP that you can establish rapport with a stranger and convince them to buy a product from you. In other words, it is a function of interpersonal skills that connect one's mental abilities, behavioral responses, and their sensitivity to feelings and outcomes achieved.

In a sales situation, it goes a long way in connecting the parties' viewpoints and their buyer-seller interaction effects. As a salesperson, to make NLP work for you in closing sales, you must pay attention to the following features;

Mental ability; in other words, you must perceive emotions accurately. You must be able to read your prospect's feelings so that you can tell the difference between hones and dishonest expressions. This will also help you mirror their emotions and take their viewpoints. It also goes a long way in helping you manage your own emotions as well as those of others.

Behavioral response; is one that is concerned with how you relate and connect with others. This includes various aspects such as communication output your client may be sending either verbally, non-verbally, or through their tonal voices.

Mutual feelings sensitivity; is one feature that is concerned with how you interact and your ability to sense your surroundings. Can you tell me whether the atmosphere is pleasant? Does it foster a sense of trust and friendship between you and your prospect? Having a high mutual feeling sensitivity also allows you to change the atmosphere using humor, among other strategies, so that it is warm and welcoming to your target audience.

Interaction outcome achievability; is a feature that is mainly concerned with your ability to achieve the desired outcome – close sales. For instance, it might mean you are getting relevant information that will help you get through to your buyer and get them to behave in a particular manner. This may also mean that you have to conform to their way of life just so that you can get the desired outcome.

All these skills are what are carried out at the conscious level. The key in NLP is to create a long-term buyer-seller relationship and not just a one-off experience. By the time you are through reading this book, you will have understood;

- How to communicate with impact
- Establish rapport with your target clients to inculcate a long-lasting relationship
- How to add powerful listening skills that will help you in identifying relevant buyer signals
- How to correctly interpret your clients' needs, wants as well as their buying patterns
- How your prospects prefer to be treated throughout the sales process

So, what are you still waiting for? Start putting all these techniques, tips, and tricks into practice and watch how your sales closing soars this year.

Happy selling!

Acknowledgments

I would like to take this opportunity to thank the Universe as well as everybody who has touched my life. This book is the result of over four decades of experience, learning, practicing, researching, and failing many times in the area of sales. I would like to thank my first batch of 20 students of Public Speaking Mastery. I inspired all of them to write a book in their subject of specialization. As a coach and trainer, I also committed to the group that I will also finish a book during the course within three months. We all did it, and all of us are going to launch our books on 1st of February 2020.

Here are the names of the participant of my first batch, and these are very special to me because of their trust in me to join my 3 months public speaking course and inspiring me to write this book.

Sushil Rajput

Nirvan Sharma

Shailender Arora

Amit Chaturvedi

Ishita Bhardwaj

Sanjeev Jaitly

Dr. Angela Sharma

Dr. Rinki Srivastav

Dr. Amit Verma

Dr. Prabha Singh

Dr. Pankaj Bharti

Dr. Hitesh Khurana

Ashmit Bhardwaj

Sanjiv Arora

Krishan Mohan Sharma

Pavan Sachdev

Dinesan K

Anant Kasibhatla

Arun Mishra

Mukesh Pandey

Last, but not least, I thank my wife Uma, my sons Rahul and Tarun, and my daughter-in-law Deeksha, who have stood by me and have always supported and encouraged me.

www.ingramcontent.com/pod-product-compliance
Lightning Source LLC
Chambersburg PA
CBHW070437220526
45466CB00004B/1719